Beyond the Blue Polo

A Daughter's Journey Through Love, Loss, and Legacy

by Lennidies Montanez

Beyond the Blue Polo – A Daughter's Journey Through Love, Loss and Legacy

Published by LM Stories & Co.
Hollywood, Florida

Cover design by Lennidies Montanez
Printed in the United States of America

Dedication

For my parents,

Milagros and Nestor —

The light that guided me home.

Dear Dad,

Not a day goes by that I do not think of you. I miss hearing your voice, your laugh, the way you filled our home with warmth and quiet joy. There are still moments when I turn a corner and expect to see you sitting at your desk, typing your poems, or asking what is for dinner. Those little things—your routines, your humor, your presence—made our home feel alive in a way words can hardly describe.

Having you with us was one of the greatest blessings of my life. Luis and I often talk about how much you added to our days, how our house became more than walls and rooms; it became a space filled with love, laughter, and purpose. You made our home complete. Even in the hard moments, we saw God's hand guiding us, shaping our days with meaning and grace.

I am so grateful that you are with Mom again, that you are both whole and at peace. I picture you together—no more pain, no more confusion, just light and love and laughter like before. It brings me comfort knowing you are exactly where you wanted to be, watching over us.

Our journey was beautifully and wonderfully made by God. Through caring for you, I learned strength I did not know I had and faith I did not know I could live. You showed me what resilience, grace, and unconditional love truly look like.

Your old room—the one where you wrote your poetry and where you took your final breath—is now my office and studio. It is where I create my candles and my art. The light that shines through that space still feels like you. Every time I work there, I feel your presence guiding me, reminding me that love and creativity never fade, they simply transform.

Your poem Lovely House! could not describe us more perfectly. This house, this life, is filled with your spirit. It is, and will always be, our lovely house.

Thank you for every lesson, every memory, every moment. You are forever my hero, my teacher, and my heart.

With all my love, Nini (Lennidies Montanez)

The Story

Beyond the Blue Polo: A Daughter's Journey Through Caregiving, Loss, and Legacy

Table of Contents

Prologue

The camera caught him again — pockets full of sugar-free cookies, crumbs scattered across his shirt like tiny confetti. If you asked him, he had not touched a thing.

That was Dad — equal parts stubborn, charming, and mischievous. Caring for him in his final years was like raising a toddler who could write poetry, fix a leaky faucet, and win an argument without saying much at all. It was exhausting, hilarious, and, looking back now, one of the greatest privileges of my life.

Most days, he wore his favorite blue polo shirt. He had plenty of clothes, but somehow that shirt won every time. Ninety degrees outside? Blue polo. Family birthday party? Blue polo. A trip to the doctor? You guessed it. I used to think it was stubbornness, but now I know it was comforting, his armor in a world that kept changing around him.

Two days after his last birthday, I sat beside him, holding his hand as his breathing slowed. The room was still — the kind of quiet you do not forget. In that moment, all the memories came rushing in — cookie crumbs, the blue polo, the way he could vanish from a waiting room like a magician — and the three symbols that marked our journey: the forget-me-not for the dementia that slowly blurred our days, the red tulip for the Parkinson's that challenged his every step, and the orange ribbon for the kidney cancer that tested us one more time. These were not just illnesses; they were chapters in the story of his resilience.

That magician trick was classic Dad. It happened during the pandemic when he had an ultrasound appointment. I had told the staff he was a wanderer, parked my car right outside, and waited for the call to pick him up. Then the door opened, and there he was — walking out, smiling like a man who had better places to be. "They were taking too long," he said, as if that explained everything. And somehow, it did.

For the laughter that kept us going, for the tears we could not hold back, and for the truth that makes both matter even more — two days after his 78th birthday, he passed away peacefully at home — this book is for him.

The Matriarch's Legacy and Remembering Mom

 My mother, Milagros, was the anchor of our family — a woman whose warmth could fill a room and whose quiet strength guided us through life's storms. She taught us the value of family, of showing up for each other even when it was inconvenient or hard. Losing her in April 2013 was like losing the center of gravity in my world.

She and Dad had a love that was not loud, but it was steady. They moved through life as partners in every sense, building a home where laughter and hard work lived side by side. When she passed, I knew that Dad's life would never be the same. What I did not know was that, in many ways, mine would not either.

It was in those first months without her that I began to understand what caregiving truly meant — not as a concept, but as a commitment you make from the deepest place in your heart.

Before she was my mother, Milagros was a girl shaped by faith and discipline. She was raised in a Catholic home and, as she often told us, went to Catholic school all the way through college. The lessons were simple and steady, work hard, tell the truth, help people, show up. She was "raised right," as they would say, and you could feel it in the way she carried herself and cared for others.

There is a photo I keep coming back to—she is in a white gown, radiant and composed, what looks like a sweet-15 or sweet-16 portrait. She is breathtaking. That was my mother: always put together, always stunning, beauty inside and out. It is easy to see why my father fell in love with her. She was a good human first, and she was also beautiful.

What I remember most now, looking back, is her resilience. Even when she was exhausted, she kept going—for us. Through life's struggles and her own health challenges, she showed up. That was her love language: showing up, again. It hurts to live without her, because we did not just lose a mother—we lost one of the greatest women we have ever known.

In 1984, her strength found its fiercest test. My dad suffered a stroke and an aneurysm, and my mother became his rock even while she was breaking. He needed everything—therapy appointments, patience, a second chance at the basics of living—and she gave it all. Dad had to learn life over again, and when his frustration boiled into raised voices, she absorbed it, steady and unshaken. She became the full-time caregiver, the quiet force holding our family together, and she sheltered us so that what we saw was the father who remained strong. Only now do I realize she was also preparing me—training my heart for the unthinkable years later.

The Gentle Giant's Resilience and Stepping into the Role

 Dad, Nestor, was a quiet man in many ways, but his presence filled a room. He had a calm, steady way about himself, the kind of person who did not need to speak loudly to be heard. His resilience was a trait I admired even before illness tested it.

He was born in Puerto Rico, just like Mom, and he carried that island grit and warmth wherever he went. In the old photos of the two of them, he is handsome and sure, a force beside her. The love between them is obvious in every frame. He did not share much about his childhood, but I know he was adopted and spent years searching for his biological mother. He did find her later in life, and though the reunion was not what he hoped for, it told me everything about the strength it takes to seek the truth and make peace with what you find. By fifteen, he was out on his own, already shaping himself into the man he would become.

What I remember most is his hands—how they could fix and build anything. Dad was an entrepreneur at heart. He loved houses not as they were, but as they could be. Renovation was his language. There is a family story about a three-story home in Rhode Island they bought for one dollar. It needed everything. He gave it everything. I have photos of that house—from when we lived there, from after we moved, and even now, years later. She is still standing. That was Dad: a fixer who turned neglect into possibility, ruined into refuge.

When Mom passed, I stepped into a new role in his life. I was not just his daughter anymore; I became his advocate, his companion, and eventually, his caregiver. That shift was not something I planned, but it was something I embraced, even when it was exhausting. Watching a man who could repair anything face a body he could no longer "fix" was its own heartbreak. Still, the same quiet resolve that rebuilt houses showed up in him—one appointment at a time, one exhausting day at a time.

I learned quickly that resilience is not about never feeling tired or overwhelmed, it is about continuing to show up even when you are. Dad taught me that long before I realized I was learning it. He built homes; later, we built a different kind of shelter together made of patience, advocacy, and love.

"The Trilogy of Strength, Faith, and Love"

The forget-me-nots, the red tulips, and the orange ribbon became my symbols for this journey — each one carrying its own meaning, its own season of love and letting go. The forget-me-nots reminded me of memory and the ache of fading moments. The red tulips taught me about grace and beauty in decline. And the orange ribbon, bright and unwavering, came to represent courage — the strength to keep showing up, to keep believing, even when life felt heavy. Together, they became my trilogy of strength, faith, and enduring love.

Forget-Me-Nots and the Falls: When Memory and Strength Begin to Fade

As Dad's dementia progressed, one of the hardest battles we faced was keeping him safe from himself…It started subtly. A misplaced set of keys, a story repeated twice in the same conversation. At first, I chalked it up to age, to normal forgetfulness. But as the months went on, the gaps widened. He would relive Mom's death repeatedly or ask whether he had eaten breakfast.

What I understand now is that the forgetting began with grief. After Mom died, Dad was unmoored. He did not often grieve in front of others, but at home—just the two of us had long, quiet talks. He missed her. He missed their routine. He missed the simple fact of her. After almost fifty years of marriage, she was gone, and he was devastated.

He told and retold the story of finding her, his voice looping like a record, not realizing he was speaking to her daughter, their daughter—who had lost her mother, too. Those first months were brutal. My job was to be there because that is what he needed. As the stories kept returning, other things slipped away. The holes in his memory widened, and I learned to walk around them with him.

There were moments I will never forget: catching him standing in front of her photos, tears in his eyes, whispering, "Why did she leave me? Why isn't she coming back for me? Why am I here?" Sometimes he could not remember, and sometimes he remembered too much, lost in a past that felt safer than the present—back in Puerto Rico with Mom, my youngest brother still in her belly, a whole life in front of them. I would cry quietly, calling out to my mother in my own heart: Why did you leave me?

The forget-me-not became my private symbol for this stage of our journey, a tiny bloom that says, Hold on. Remember. It reminded me that while memory may fade, love does not. Caring for someone with dementia means holding their history for them, protecting their dignity when the mind lets go, and choosing gentleness even when the day is hard. It meant answering the same questions as if for the first time, building small anchors—a photo on the fridge, a note on the table, breakfast at the same hour—so the day had edges he could find.

I learned to meet him where he was, not where I wanted him to be. If he were in 1973, I would have gone to 1973 with him. If he was waiting for Mom, I sat with that waiting. The point was not to correct the past out of him, but to keep the present kind. In those moments, the forget-me-not was not just a flower—it was a promise: I will remember for us, and I will love you through the forgetting.

As Dad's dementia deepened, right before hospice, he entered a phase that was both heartbreaking and oddly humorous — he decided he needed to hide everything. He would tuck things away in drawers, under papers, in boxes, and sometimes in the most random places. It was his way of holding on to control, of trying to keep his world in order even as his mind unraveled.

After he passed, I began the painful process of cleaning out his closet. I was folding his clothes, tears falling, when I reached for his pants. As I lifted one pair, something heavy clanked inside the pocket. Then another. I reached in — and found one of his old CDs. Then another. And another. He had hidden all his favorite music in his pant pockets, as if to keep them close, safe from disappearing.

In that moment, I laughed through my tears. It was such a funny, bittersweet discovery — a reminder of the chaos that dementia creates, but also of the beautiful, childlike logic that lived inside him until the end. Even in confusion, Dad's music was his comfort, his secret joy tucked quietly away in a place he thought no one would find.

"Dignity isn't about never falling — it's about always getting back up."

Red Tulips – Balancing Grace and Decline

There is a reason I chose red tulips to mark this season of our journey. Tulips are graceful even as they bow, vibrant even as they fade. They remind me of the balance between dignity and decline— the quiet beauty that remains when strength begins to slip. Caring for Dad during these months meant learning to see that grace, to find color in moments that felt gray, and to honor his independence while accepting that he was changing before my eyes. When the Parkinson's diagnosis came, it felt like another door closing. His hands, once so steady, began to tremble. His gait slowed. Everyday tasks turned into deliberate, careful movements. I cannot pinpoint the exact date—only that it was after the 1984 incident. Mom met at this stage of their journey with the same steel she had shown before.

What followed was a maze of doctors and medication trial and error, side effects that sometimes felt worse than the symptoms. Some medications made the tremors rage; others dulled him or unsettled his sleep. It was frustrating for both until, slowly, the right combination gave him a measure of control. Even then, the anger would surface—not at us, but at a body that would not obey. He hid his hands when they shook; if his shoulder trembled, he pressed a palm against it, trying to still what would not be stilled. Once he told me, "This is the worst thing a man can go through—not having control of his own body." I have never forgotten that.

When Dad moved to Florida, we started over. I found him a new primary doctor and, right away, a neurologist to review his medications. All I had were the bottles he brought with him, and I needed to be sure he was in the right plan. I still feel a spark of anger about that transition—not at anyone, but at the reality that this would be our new norm: managing, adjusting, advocating all over again. The neurologist decided to take him off his meds to reassess what he needed and at what dosages. It was awful. Neither of us slept that night. His whole-body shook, relentless, and we ended up making an emergency visit just to make him comfortable. I remember sitting there in disbelief that this was even possible, learning in real time how vigilant I would have to be for him.

The red tulip—the international symbol of Parkinson's—came to stand for more than a diagnosis. It came to mean grace under constraint. Dad rarely complained. He adjusted, one day at a time, teaching me patience in the slow rhythm of dressing, buttoning, eating, walking. We learned to plan for good hours and hard hours, to celebrate small victories: a steady spoonful of soup, a walk to the mailbox, a night of uninterrupted sleep. In the quiet work of accepting what was, he showed me a different kind of strength— one that does not roar but endures.

The Orange Ribbon: The Battle You Don't Choose

The orange ribbon became a symbol of Dad's fight — vibrant, determined, and full of courage. It was not a ribbon of pity, but of purpose. Each time I saw that color, I thought of strength, of endurance, of the light that burns even in exhaustion. For me, it came to represent the battles we do not choose but are called to fight — the courage to keep showing up when hope feels distant. This part of the journey was not about winning; it was about enduring, trusting that love and faith would be enough to carry us through. I remember the day we found out. Dad was not feeling well and had a high fever. Not wanting to take any chances, my husband and I took him to the emergency room.

While undergoing testing, the doctor came in and, without much preamble, said, "With your diagnosis of kidney cancer, you will need to see a nephrologist and your primary doctor to get treatment." Dad did not catch what the doctor had said, so my husband and I stepped into the hallway and asked for clarification. The doctor explained that he had a tumor, and it needed further testing.

I was floored. While Dad understood English, I still interpreted it into Spanish for him. That was the moment our cancer journey began.

Mom, who had already passed, would be spared this new emotional roller coaster. But for me, it was the beginning of another chapter in caregiving — one that would demand even more strength and resolve.

The days after that diagnosis were a blur — a mix of medical appointments, quiet prayers, and the slow realization that life as we knew it had changed forever. Despite recognizing the challenges that lay before us, it was clear that our only option was to confront them side by side.

The Journey Begins: Building a New Normal

When Dad first came to live with us in Florida in April 2013, just days after Mom passed away, I knew life was about to change — but I did not know how much. We had lived apart for years, visiting often, but having him in our home full-time was different.

It was a season of adjustment. The house felt both fuller and quieter at the same time. Full of his presence — his footsteps in the hallway, his voice calling from the living room — but quieter because Mom's absence was felt in every corner.

I became his constant. I made the appointments, refilled the medications, and kept the fridge stocked with his favorite snacks. But caregiving is not just about logistics. It is about learning a new rhythm together, and we were finding ours — one day at a time.

In December 2017, life shifted again. I was diagnosed with Myasthenia Gravis, a rare neuromuscular disease that brought fatigue, weakness, and fear into my everyday life. There were plasma exchanges, long hospital stays, and mornings when I could not even brush my own hair.

And yet, through all of that, I still made sure Dad got to his appointments, took his medications, and felt safe in our home. I did not do it alone — my husband and children were my steady anchors — but I learned a new kind of strength, the kind that is built in the quiet moments between exhaustion and love.

Then came the pandemic when hospitals and clinics closed their doors to family members. During one of Dad's regular ultrasound appointments — after his kidney tumor removal — I reminded the nurse, "He has dementia and likes to wander. Please keep someone with him." She smiled and assured me she would. I waited in the car, nervous but trusting.

About forty-five minutes later, I looked up and saw him — walking right out of the building, smiling, heading down the sidewalk as if nothing were wrong. I followed for a moment before calling out his name.

"I was tired of waiting in that cold room," he said, his voice calm, as if that explained everything.

I could not help but laugh, though my heart was racing. I canceled the rest of the appointment and found another clinic. That moment stayed with me — a mix of fear, relief, and deep understanding. Dementia has a way of evaluating your faith in both patience and timing.

Even amid uncertainty and constant adjustments, there were sparks of light — small reminders that laughter and connection still lived in our home. Those moments became my anchor, pulling me back to joy when the days grew heavy.

Photo: Exterior of ultrasound clinic —where dad wandered away from...

Blue Polo Moments – Humor and Dignity in the Small Things

One of my favorite memories was the day my husband pulled Dad into a TikTok challenge. It was one of those videos where you bang on pots and pans, chanting "I want food!" until someone gives in. Only in our case, they wanted coffee. My husband was in perfect rhythm, but Dad was gloriously out of sync, banging away at his own tempo. The chaos made it even funnier, and the kitchen was filled with laughter.

Humor like that was our lifeline — it lightened the heaviness of caregiving and kept Dad engaged and connected. Even when the days were long, moments like these gave us the strength to keep going.

Looking back, those bursts of joy were more than just comic relief — they were lessons in their own right. They taught me that love is not just shown in grand gestures, but in the small, imperfect moments that make life worth remembering.

Some of my favorite memories were the mornings when my grandchildren stayed over. They would argue about who would get to help me feed Great-Grandpa his breakfast — usually his favorite, French toast — or who would bring him his morning medication. Dad loved those moments, especially when his great-granddaughter proudly carried in his breakfast tray while his great-grandson followed behind with his medicine, both serious and focused, but giggling the whole time.

These were priceless moments that will never be taken away. And then there were the other great grandkids, the ones who would run down the hall and burst into his room as if to announce, *"I'm here!"* They would play with his things, move his papers, tap his keyboard

— and, though Dad would sigh and pretend to be bothered, his eyes always softened. He loved every bit of their energy, even when he tried to hide it. Those moments filled our home with laughter, noise, and the kind of life that reminded me of how love truly lives in the small, ordinary days. "Those mornings reminded me that love is never one generation deep — it keeps showing up, tray in hand, ready to serve."

And in a way that only God could weave together, those same two great grandkids later stood beside their mother and aunt to sing at his funeral. The same little voices that once filled his room with laughter now filled the church with song. It was as if the circle had closed — the joy, love, and the faith he left behind returning to honor him one last time.

"That circle of family, laughter, and faith would continue to hold me long after he was gone"?

Photo: Dad and Luis banging on the pans – TikTok challenge...

The Circle That Carried Us

During those years, I was never truly alone in caring for Dad. God placed some remarkable people in our lives—angels in everyday clothes—who loved him as their own.

Our pastor would randomly stop by the house, unannounced but always right on time. He would spend an hour or more sitting with Dad, talking about Scripture, laughing about life, or simply letting Dad cry in a safe space. I never had to ask. He would just call and say, "Has your dad eaten lunch yet?" and then show up with something delicious and two forks. They would share a meal and easy conversation, and I would see a light in Dad's eyes that only genuine companionship could spark.

My sister-in-law called him "Mr. [expletive] Rhode Island," a nickname that made him grin every single time. She was straightforward and real with him, never sugar-coating a thing, and he loved that about her. The day she came to visit was priceless; he told me afterward it felt like seeing an old friend who knew exactly how to make him laugh.

Then there was a dear family friend—more like a daughter than anything else—who watched over him whenever my husband and I managed a rare bit of time away. She gave him his medications, made him home-cooked meals, tucked him in, and simply was there. Her presence brought me peace and gave him comfort.

Each of my children found their own quiet ways to connect. They would stop by to talk with him, help with small tasks, or just keep him company. My daughters-in-law were here for me but also for him, bringing warmth and laughter into the house when we both needed it most.

To every one of these unsung heroes—thank you. You gave us time, love, patience, and grace. You made this journey lighter and reminded me that caregiving is never meant to be done alone. You were God's hands in motion.

Photo: Family gathering at home...

The Falls and the Fight for Independence

As Dad's dementia progressed, one of the hardest battles we faced was keeping him safe from himself. He could not understand that he could no longer walk without his walker. It was so frustrating—not because of him, but because of how determined he was to stay independent. He would get up fast to go to the bathroom, and we would hear a thump from his room, right next to ours. My husband and I would rush in to find him on the floor, confused, his eyebrow or cheek often bloody. And somehow, every time, he would smile as if to tell us, "It's okay, don't worry."

There were a few morning trips to the emergency room, and I would take pictures so I could show him later how bad the falls were. He would look, shake his head, and laugh— "Another scar for the books," he would say, brushing it off like it was nothing.

He argued constantly about the walker and the cane. "I don't need it," he would say, his pride stronger than his balance. The nurses who came to help were just as persistent as I was, though. I remember one day so clearly—the nurse came for his scheduled exercise walk. He did not want to go; all he wanted was to stay in his room, his refuge, and type on his computer. But he needed to move, so she helped him with his sneakers (which he hated), adjusted the walker, and went out.

I stood by the doorway and took a short video to send to my siblings—I am not sure if I ever did. There was Dad, walking too fast, leaning to the left, ready to fall. The nurse kept telling him, "Slow down, Mr. Matias," and he just kept going, stubborn as ever. Finally, he lifted the walker off the ground completely, wobbling his way back toward the house. When they got back, he told her he was done and to go home. She left, and I sat with him at the kitchen

27

table while he drank his coffee, retelling the story his way—with laughter and pride, turning frustration into another one of his adventures.

The silent frustration was real. He needed help. I needed help. But through it all, his determination—and that ability to find humor even in the hardest moments—reminded me that dignity is not about never falling. It is about always getting back up.

Photo: Dad walking too fast with nurse.

A Christmas in Georgia

One year we decided to spend Christmas in Georgia, at my husband's brother's house. It was a beautiful home—big, warm, and full of laughter. Two of my three sons came with their families, and a few of our friends from church made the trip as well. We drove there, Dad, my husband, and me in our car long ride full of stories, laughter, and a few wrong turns that still make me smile.

Dad was the champion. His dementia was not too bad yet, and we thought we had everything under control. We were wrong.

The first night was awful. My husband's brother had set up a bedroom for Dad on the main floor, right next to a bathroom. My husband and I slept on an air mattress in the living room nearby so we could hear him if he needed anything. Somehow, in the middle of the night, Dad ended up in the garage—lost, confused, and wandering. We found him there among some toppled boxes. He insisted he had not fallen, but he was fibbing a little to spare us the worry. Thankfully, he was not hurt.

That night made me realize just how much routine meant to him. Being in an unfamiliar house had thrown him off completely. He did not know where the bathroom was, which door led to where, and it scared him as much as it scared us. I remember sitting with him afterward, holding his hand, both of us too tired to sleep.

The truth is, Dad was never very sociable. Even before his dementia worsened, he preferred the comfort of home to big family gatherings. A few times, he would travel to Naples to visit one of my brothers, but those trips stopped quickly because the long drive wore him out. He skipped Thanksgiving dinners at my son's house because he did not want to travel—and honestly, he had always been that way. Mom used to laugh about it, saying that Dad loved people but did not love crowds.

That is what made the Georgia trip so special. Despite his hesitation, he came with us—and for those few days, he opened himself up to joy again. He played with the great grandkids, ate well, and laughed with everyone. He finally got much-needed rest, and we shared a Christmas filled with warmth and gratitude—one I will always remember as the Christmas we made it work, together.

When He Stayed in His Room

Even before his dementia grew worse, Dad had always been more comfortable in his own space. He loved people, but he did not love being around too many of them. There were so many times when we would have gatherings at the house—birthdays, holidays, dinners—and he would stay in his room instead of joining us.

I can still picture him sitting by his desk, typing away on his computer, the sound of keys tapping softly behind a closed door. Sometimes he would leave the shades open just enough to see what was happening outside. I remember the day of my oldest son's wedding—held right there in our home. Everyone was dressed up, music was playing, laughter filled every corner—but Dad stayed in his room. I looked toward his window and saw him there, just watching quietly through the glass, his face half-lit by the computer screen.

I wish I had taken a picture of that moment. It was not sadness, but it was exactly more like peace. That was his way of being part of the world, on his own terms. Even from his room, he was present writing, thinking, watching, loving us from a distance.

A Song for Grandpa

There was another moment I will never forget. My niece Erica traveled all the way from Rhode Island to visit her grandfather. She came into his room, sat gently on the edge of his bed, and began to play her guitar. Her voice filled the room—soft, clear, and full of love.

Dad watched her with the sweetest expression, completely still, as if taking in every word and every note. It was such a tender moment—one that reminded me how music can reach places that words cannot.

I know I took a picture but cannot find it, but the memory is one I will always treasure. It captures the quiet connection between them—the joy, peace, and the way love finds its own language when spoken through song.

How Great Thou Art

One Sunday after church, our little group came back to the house to spend the afternoon together. My daughter-in-law and the young woman I lovingly call my "other daughter" began to sing one of Dad's favorite songs— "How Great Thou Art" by Carrie Underwood.

Right there in the middle of my living room, surrounded by family and friends, they sang. The sound filled the air—tender, powerful, and full of love. Two of my brothers were there that day with some of their families, and we all just stood still, listening. You could feel gratitude, the reverence, the sense that this moment was something more than just music. It was worship.

Dad sat quietly, his eyes closed, a faint smile on his face. We all knew we were witnessing something special—one of those rare, sacred pauses in life when you can feel God's presence moving among you.

When the song ended, no one spoke. We just held that silence like a prayer.

Later, at Dad's funeral, they sang "How Great Thou Art" again as he was lowered into the ground. That song has never sounded the same since—it carries both joy and ache, comfort, and longing. Every time I hear it now, I think of that day in my living room, a room filled with voices, faith, and the kind of love that never fades.

Words He Made His Own

My father's poetry was his way of finding light in the quiet—his words were his prayers. Writing became his refuge, his way of remembering, and his way of teaching me that love does not fade, it transforms.

In the years before his passing, Dad's poems were featured in national anthologies published by Poetry.com. His poem "Lovely House!" appeared as the first poem in the collection Timeless Voices (edited by Howard Ely), a reflection of the warmth, hope, and love he poured into every verse. His words also appeared in Surrender to the Moon, another anthology of poets sharing their hearts and reflections on life.

The following poems are selections he cherished, rewrote, or created during his final years, each one quiet conversation between faith and memory. The first one is his own creation, and it was published.

The following poems Today, Big Family, I wish you were here and when my time comes were all scanned from my father's binders of poems.

Lovely House!

A lovely house is not really
four square walls with pictures hung up.
A house is where someone always waits for you!

And where all the memories come free,
surrounded with perfect and beautiful scenes.
A house is where you breathe,
peace and honesty . . .

And a house is not merely roof and rooms,
but is like walking in the clouds through the hallways,
and where a dear love gives you kisses
under the moonlight . . .

But what is a house without anybody to meet
or welcome you when the day is done?
A house is sweet, imaginably sweet!

Originally published under the name Matias Nestor

Reprinted with love and remembrance of Nestor Matias

From Timeless Voices, edited by Howard Ely (The International
Library of Poetry, 2003)

Today!

Author: Nestor Matias

Today I remember when you,
held ours childs when I comes home,
from work and the threasured times,
like these when we grew into a family..........

We were young then with just,
a litle experience at that time but so,
involve in love each other but ours love,
endured the pains and heartached of,
the universe but that keeps us strong...........

I also remember when we grieved,
ours loss, with parents gone and feeling,
lost, but stil ours love never being touch,
thru pains and heartaches we stil deal,
with a bad situations and throubles.............

And if we did right or wrong only,
ours heavenly father have the answer,
I only know in my heart that in my dear,
arms I do belong as well her on mine!~

Big Family!

Author: Nestor Matias

My wife and I were so young,
as we start a family together,
there were a little trouble as we,
start ours relation down the road.........

But we manage to deal with it,
cause we we were strong all the,
way thru the task trying to keep,
all of ourself together.................

And pretty soon we become,
a big and strong family of seven,
my wife were a strong healthy,
woman, and me a happy long ranger...........

We were please to see ours childrens,
grow steady and happy along and theirs,
childrens as well forever and ever, Iam,
walking slow now like forgiven the time,
and weather by now!~~

I Wish You Were Here!

Author: Nestor Matias

Every moment I remember you,
I can not forget you or keep you apart,
of my side dear, is impossible for me,
living my life this way, because I feel,
you in every move I make...........................

You always are present on my mind,
I feel you in my verse and my poems as,
well, cause you live on my heart and do,
not paid any rent now or ever...................

But this morning I wish you were here,
many years have fade away since you die,
and can not forget that day when they take
your body out of the house something I never,
see it before on my long life dear....................

And believe me dear is hurt even to think,
about, like an open wound deep on the heart,
but there is days I don't feel like chat with not,
one, because Iam not in the mood to talk about,
my life, what life, my life ends when you die!~~

When My Time Comes!

Author: Nestor Matias

Last night I feel I was walking,
down the road with Jesus,
then I realize I was there for a reason,
to perform an inportant task..............

I was lonely wonderrer and searching,
for a place to belong and feel safe also,
a place to call home sweet home,
were words counts the most.................

But long time ago I have my trails
in life, even a few brief spots of separations,
and Jesus comes to my heart,
like not one before to rescue me..................

And since them I feel safe and confortable,
but something were wrong sadly my dear love,
suddenly she is gone and I can be with her anymore,
but I hope when my time comes she came with Jesus,
to carry me away this I wait inpatient every day!~~

Notes on the Poems

In his later years, Dad found comfort in poetry—both in writing his own verses and in drawing inspiration from the words of others.

Several of the pieces in this section were included in anthologies published by Poetry.com, where his work and artist profile appeared alongside poets from around the world. The collections that featured his writing include:

• Timeless Voices — Edited by Howard Ely, Poetry.com

• Surrender to the Moon — Edited by Howard Ely, Poetry.com

Each poem in this section was reimagined and rewritten in his voice, often changing the titles and verses to reflect his own experiences and feelings. As his dementia grew his thoughts were these were his. I give all my thanks to the poetry community which my father loved so much

Afterword: What Caregiving Taught Me About Living

Reflecting on my experiences, I understand that caregiving was not just a task assigned to me—it played a significant role in shaping my identity. It tested me, refined me, and softened me all at once. There were moments when I felt strong and steady, and others when I did not know how I would make it through the day. But through it all, I learned that love is not just shown through big gestures — it is found in the quiet, ordinary acts of care that often go unseen.

Caring for Dad changed the way I see time. Every routine — making coffee, folding blankets, adjusting his pillow, sitting quietly beside him — became sacred. Those small moments were holy ground. They taught me patience, compassion, and presence in ways I had never known before.

I also learned that faith is not about having all the answers. It is about trusting that God is there in every uncertain moment — in every fall, every tear, every laugh, and every goodbye. Through caregiving, I learned that love does not end when life does. It continues, reshaping itself into memory, into legacy, into strength.

In those last days, the sound of the oxygen machine became part of our home — a steady rhythm, a constant reminder of breath and life. At night, I could hear it humming softly through the walls, its pulse filling the silence. It was strange how something mechanical could sound so alive, as if the house itself were breathing with him.

We were waiting for the hospice nurse to tell us it was time. Those nurses were my angels — for my rest, for my sanity, and for my transition into letting go. Their presence brought peace to the house and gave me space to just be a daughter again, not only a caregiver.

That evening, I called my siblings and asked them to speak to Dad. Even though he could not respond, I needed them to say their goodbyes. I did not think they would make it on time, and I could not bear for their words to go unheard. So, one by one, they spoke to him through the phone — voices filled with love, gratitude, and tears. It was as if each word carried him a little closer to peace.

On the night Dad took his final breath, Luis was by my side. We had both been keeping watch, quiet, holding space for peace to come gently. When that moment arrived, a single tear fell from Dad's right eye. It was so painful, yet so peaceful — as if his body wept goodbye while his spirit rose home. Luis and I still talk about that moment. It was both heartbreak and holiness — the end of one journey and the beginning of another.

Dad gave me more than I could ever give him. His courage, humor, and stubborn spirit taught me resilience. His writing reminded me that words can heal. And his presence — even in silence — taught me that we can find grace in both holding on and letting go.

Now, when I walk into the room that once belonged to him — my studio, my creative space — I feel his peace there. It is where I create, where I remember, and where I thank God for the gift of a life that was beautifully and wonderfully made.

Caregiving did not just teach me how to help someone live well — it taught me how to love deeply, how to forgive freely, and how to keep my heart open, even when it hurts.

And sometimes, when the house is still, I can almost hear the hum of that oxygen machine again — a quiet rhythm that reminds me love never really leaves; it just changes form and keeps breathing through us.

Epilogue: Finding Peace and A Legacy of Love

 Two days after his 78th birthday, Dad passed away peacefully at home. The house was quiet in a way I had never heard before. In that stillness, I felt the weight of loss, but also the comfort of knowing I had been there for him in every way I could.

His blue polo hung in the closet, untouched. I could not bring myself to move it, not yet. It was more than just a shirt — it was a symbol of his strength, his stubbornness, and his comfort in a changing world.

I like to think that he left this world knowing how deeply he was loved. And I left that chapter of my life knowing that caregiving, though it tested me in every way, also shaped me into the person I was meant to be.

Notation: Together Forever/A few memories

Memories

Memories

Memories

Memories

Author's Note: A Tribute to Enduring Love

This book is a love letter — to my father, Nestor, to my mother,
Milagros, and to the countless caregivers who walk this path.
May you find comfort in knowing that your work matters, that
your love is felt, and that the moments you share — even the hard
ones — are part of a legacy that will outlast you.

I wrote *The Blue Polo Book* to honor my parents and to offer
comfort to anyone walking a similar road. If you are caring for
someone you love, know that you are not alone. May these pages
remind you that love is patient, presence is powerful, and that the
smallest moments often hold the deepest meaning.

— *Lennidies*

Acknowledgments

To my husband, Luis — your love carried us. You gave Dad baths, cut his hair, fed him, and sat up on the long nights when I could not. You cared for him with a tenderness that went beyond duty — it was friendship, devotion, and love in its truest form. You never wavered, not once. When Dad passed, you were there beside me. We watched as he took his last breath, and a single tear fell from his right eye — a moment we still talked about, both painful and peaceful, a final gesture of love that we will never forget. When you said you had lost your best friend, I knew how deeply that bond ran. Thank you for standing beside both of us with strength, patience, and grace.

To my middle son, who shared our home and lived this journey with us day by day — thank you for your patience, your gentle humor, and your calm voice when Dad grew restless. You carried so much of the daily weight with me, often without being asked, and your quiet strength gave me comfort when I needed it most. You were not only a grandson to Dad but also a companion, a caretaker, and a reminder that love is best shown in small, faithful acts.

To my other two sons — thank you for always stepping in when we needed you most. Whether it was giving Dad his medications, helping him eat, or simply sitting with him so we could rest or travel, you were both part of his comfort and his dignity. Your willingness to show up, to love him through action, and to support us through every phase of his care meant more than words can express.

To my daughters-in-law — thank you for bringing light, laughter, and grace into our home, and for standing beside me with understanding hearts.

To my siblings — thank you for every call, every prayer, and for loving Dad in your own ways and showing up when it mattered.

To, my sister-in-law (who affectionately called him "Mr. [expletive] Rhode Island"), our daughter you know who you are – for just being you and loving on him as if he were your grandpa, our pastor and every nurse and clinician who helped us — thank you for your hands and your hearts.

And to Dad — your words, your humor, and your strength live on. For you, Dad — always and forever.

With love and gratitude,
Lennidies Montanez

Turning the Page

A poem written in reflection, by Lennidies Montanez

I have lived the chapters I was meant to live,
each one written in laughter and ache.
I've underlined the moments that mattered,
and turned the rest over to grace.

The ink is dry on yesterday,
but the story isn't done.
Every sunrise writes a sentence
the night could never undo.

So I close this book with steady hands,
heart open, not afraid —
for endings are just whispers saying,
"There's more yet to be made."

Beyond the Blue Polo continues… in every act of love that remains.